TIME TRAVELLING TO
1972

RELIVING A VERY SPECIAL YEAR

TIME TRAVELLING TO 1972

Author
Funlighter Hub

Design
Gonçalo Sousa

December 2021

ISBN: 9798781767243

Reliving the culture, the people, the World events and the art that made 1972 a magnificent year!

Contents

SPACE EXPLORATION: The Blue Marble' That Is Earth

'Blue Marble': That was the name given by the press to the iconic photograph of the Earth that was taken on December 7th, 1972. The photo was taken by crew from inside the Apollo 17 spacecraft en route to the Moon. It was taken at a distance of about 29,000 kilometers or 18,000 miles above the Earth. It would become the first full, illuminated view of Earth in which continents and islands could be made out. The effect was astonishing.

The photo only came to attention ten days after Apollo 17 had safely landed back on Earth. A film technician named Dick Underwood at Johnson Space Center knew the photo was remarkable. The 'Blue Marble' photo was an instant sensation, being reproduced on the front page of nearly every newspaper worldwide.

The Apollo 17 crew weren't even supposed to be looking out the window at the time, since taking photos was meticulously planned as a minor part of a rigorous flight plan that detailed every single step essential to the mission. But it was just over five hours into the flight and one of the astronauts was inspired enough by what he saw to snap four photos, one of which would be the landmark 'Blue Marble' shot. All three of the astronauts onboard, the commander, Eugene A. Cernan, Ronald E. Evans and Harrison H. Schmitt, would later claim that they took the photo! However, NASA policy is that photos are always credited to the mission and not a sole astronaut.

USA: Watergate Breaks - With A Little Burglary

What would become known as the Watergate scandal began in the early hours of June 17th, 1972, with an attempted burglary at the office of the Democratic National Committee (DNC), located in the Watergate complex in Washington, D.C. The prowlers were lurking around in the darkened offices when a security guard noticed that someone had taped over several door lock in the building. The police were called and the burglars were arrested just in time. Five men were arrested at the scene.

Left to right: James McCord, Jr., Virgilio Gonzalez, Frank Sturgis, Eugenio Martinez, and Bernard Baker

The five burglars had been caught attempting to wire-tap phones and steal documents. It transpired that this was not the first time the burglars had been in the DNC's offices. They had done the same a few weeks before in May but the wire-tapping equipment they'd installed had not worked properly, so they'd gone back in for another attempt on that fateful June morning. Nixon gave a speech to the nation in August in which he swore that he and his White House staff had not been involved in the break-in at Watergate.

It would eventually transpire that the burglary was connected to President Richard Nixon's re-election campaign, known as the Committee, to Re-elect the President, or CREEP. A relentless investigation by Washington Post reporters Bob Woodward and Carl Bernstein would reveal President Nixon's direct role in the conspiracy, and Nixon would resign on August 9th, 1974. He would be the first U.S. President in to do so whilst in office.

SPACE EXPLORATION: The Mariner 9 Probe - Mars Is Calling

Mariner 9, which was the first orbital mission by NASA to Mars, had arrived at the planet in November 1971. However, it was in January 1972 that the probe was finally able to send images of Mars back to Earth. Until then, heavy dust storms on Mars and other complications had prevented Mariner 9 from taking decent photos of the surface of the planet. Even those weather disruptions confirmed what astronomers had always suspected: Mars was often afflicted by raging dust storms.

The pictures included images of Mars' polar caps and the vast Valles Marineris canyon, as well as images of the Martian moons, Deimos and Phobos. It also captured 20 volcanoes, including what would become the iconic Olympic Mons volcano. The impact of the images emitted from Mariner 9 was immense. Mariner 9 took 7,329 pictures

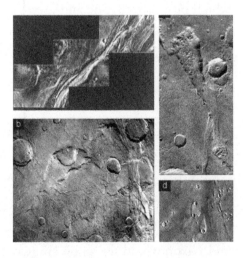

and managed to photographically map 80 percent of the surface of Mars in less than a year. Those first images during 1972 completely changed our understanding of Mars from what we thought was nothing more than a cold, crater-filled planet to realizing that it was a planet with a rich geological history and that had even once had water.

In its summary of the Mariner 9 mission, NASA stated the following: "Some of the observed features included ancient riverbeds, craters, massive extinct volcanoes, canyons, layered polar deposits, evidence of wind-driven deposition and erosion of sediments, weather fronts, ice clouds, localized dust storms, morning fogs and more".

OLYMPIC GAMES: Tragedy in the Olympic Village - 11 Israeli Hostages

The 1972 Summer Olympics in Munich, West Germany, were set to be the most modern and popular in Olympic history. However, the well-organized Games took a tragic turn in the early hours of September 5th when a group of eight Palestinian terrorists known as Black September stormed the Olympic Village apartment of the Israeli athletes. Two Israelis, wrestling coach Moshe Weinberg and weightlifter Yossef Romano, were killed in the attack. Nine other Israelis were taken hostage. The terrorists demanded that Israel release of 234 Arab prisoners being held in Israeli jails, as well as two famous German terrorists imprisoned in a West German prison, Andreas Baader and Ulrike Meinhof, the founders of the infamous Red Army Faction (RAF).

Germany was prepared to acquiesce to Black September's demands but the Israeli Prime Minister, Golda Meir, refused, saying that such kidnappings would never end if Israel agreed to the demands. In the words of Meir: "If we should give in, then no Israeli anywhere in the world can feel that his life is safe." The tense negotiations between the terrorists in the apartment and the police continued for a day. The crisis escalated in a shoot-out at Munich's airport when West German police ambushed the helicopters on which the terrorists were trying to escape.

One of the helicopters was even blown up by one of the terrorists. In the end, nine Israeli hostages were dead, as well as five terrorists and one West German policeman.

The International Olympic Committee (IOC) suspended the Munich Games for 24 hours so that memorial services could be held for the slain athletes. Quite controversially, the Games resumed after that. The Munich Massacre is still considered the darkest time in Olympic history.

NORTHERN IRELAND: 'Bloody Sunday' in Derry, Northern Ireland

On January 30th, 1972, 13 unarmed civil rights demonstrators were shot dead by British Army paratroopers in Londonderry, Northern Ireland (although the town is called Derry by local Catholics). The protesters, all of whom were Catholics, were marching in protest against the British policy of imprisoning suspected Irish nationalists being captured in Northern Ireland. British authorities had declared the march to be illegal and troops were sent in when the march went ahead. Chaos ensued and the police opened fire.

The event became known as "Bloody Sunday" and is considered one of the bloodiest events in the history of Northern Ireland. It's also considered by many as the defining point in the 'Troubles' that plagued the British province for many years.

The crisis in Northern Ireland had escalated in 1969 when British troops were sent in to suppress nationalist activity by the Irish Republican Army (IRA). The intent was also to quell mounting religious tensions and violence between Protestants and Catholics. The UK took direct control of Northern Ireland in the immediate aftermath of 'Bloody Sunday'.

Undoubtedly the iconic footage of the day was of images of Father Daly, a local Catholic priest, waving a blood-stained white handkerchief at British troops so that a mortally wounded demonstrator could be sent to hospital.

IRELAND: UK Embassy Burnt to the Ground in Dublin in Protest

The British Embassy in Merrion Square, Dublin was destroyed by fire within three days following the events of Bloody Sunday in Derry, Northern Ireland. Thousands of people protested outside the British Embassy from the very day of the massacre, whilst 100,000 people took to the streets of Dublin on February 1st, as well as dozens of other Irish cities and towns such as Cork, Waterford, Limerick and Galway.

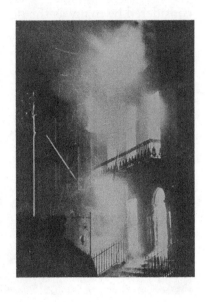

Tensions reached boiling point on February 1st, with petrol bombs and a gelignite bomb being hurled at the British Embassy. The Embassy caught fire, but fire engines were blocked by protesters for several hours. The embassy building was destroyed by the early hours of the next day.

UNITED STATES/CHINA: President Nixon Visits China

President Richard Nixon became the first U.S. president to visit the communist People's Republic of China (PRC) since it was established in 1949. He arrived in China for an official one-week trip on February 21st, 1972, in an open gambit to improve relations with the communist country at the height of the Cold War. The trip had been planned entirely in secret and the arrival of Nixon in China took everyone outside his inner circle by complete surprise. The secrecy was deemed necessary as there was fierce opposition within both countries regarding any efforts at creating ties. The efforts between the two countries became known as "ping-pong diplomacy".

During his visit, Nixon met with Chinese Premier Zhou Enlai and took an historic walk along part of the Great Wall of China with his wife, Patricia Nixon, at his side. Agreements were made to expand between the U.S. and China. Plans were also made to establish permanent U.S. trade mission in China, as well as expand cultural contacts between the two

nations. Controversially, the United States agreed to openly acknowledge that there was "One China and that Taiwan was part of China". This was a culmination of Taiwan having lost its seat at the United Nations in 1971.

UNITED NATIONS: First International Meeting on the State of the Environment

The breakthrough 1972 United Nations Conference on the Environment was held on June 5th to 16th in Stockholm, Sweden. It was the first international conference on which the natural environment of the planet was the core issue. A series of principles for improved management of the environment was agreed upon by those nations in attendance, including the Declaration and Action Plan for the Human Environment and several other resolutions.

The Stockholm Declaration contained 26 principles which placed environmental issues at the forefront of international decision-making regarding the inextricable link between economic growth and the pollution of the air, water and oceans of the world, as well as the social and mental well-being of people worldwide. There were also resolutions regarding a ban on nuclear weapon tests that may lead to radioactive

fallout and an international data bank on environmental data, among others. The first ever 'state of the environment' (SoE) report was also released, which was titled "Only One Earth," and which became the motto of the conference.

113 of the UN's 132 Member States were represented at the conference, including two heads of state: Indira Gandhi of India and Olof Palme of Sweden. There were also 250 non-governmental organizations (NGOs)

at the conference. A major and lasting outcome of the Stockholm conference was the creation of the United Nations Environment Programme (UNEP), which would have its headquarters in Nairobi, Kenya.

INTERNATIONAL RELATIONS: Richard Nixon and Leonid Brezhnev Sign SALT I

U.S. President Richard Nixon and Soviet Premier Leonid Brezhnev had undertaken a series of meetings regarding the limitation of strategic ballistic missiles by both countries. The talks began in November 1969 and an agreement was finally reached between them on May 26th, 1972, at a summit meeting in Moscow. The Strategic Arms Limitation Talks (SALT) I froze the total number of Inter-Continental Ballistic Missiles (ICBMs), but still allowed the U.S. and USSR to replace old missiles with new ones.

The SALT I talks further included other treaties and agreements:
1. The Basic Principles Agreement: This outlined important rules regarding the conduct of nuclear warfare. The two countries pledged to "do their utmost to avoid military confrontation" and that they would also "exercise restraint" in international relations, so as to prevent nuclear war as much as possible.

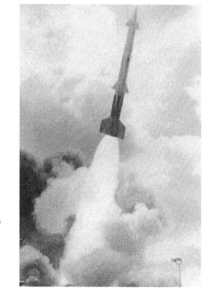

2. The ABM Treaty for anti-ballistic missile (ABM) defenses: Only 100 ABMs were allowed on each side at two sites - one site for their capital city, the other to protect their nuclear missiles.

3. The Interim Treaty: This placed limits on the number of ICBMs each country could have, namely 1618 for the USSR and 1054 for the U.S., with the Soviets getting a higher number allocated as it was agreed that the U.S. had stronger capabilities in other areas of armaments.

EAST GERMANY/WEST GERMANY: East Germany and West Germany Formally Recognize Each Other

Germany was split into two in 1949, as a result of the defeat of Nazi Germany at the end of World War II. The split resulted in the Federal Republic of Germany (FRG, or BRD in German), or West Germany, and East Germany, formally known as the German Democratic Republic (GDR, or DDR in German). The capitalist West Germany and communist East Germany had become increasingly antagonistic, especially after East Germany put up the Berlin Wall in 1961. West Germany in particular, through its Hallstein doctrine, would officially pronounce itself the only true German nation, and thus blocked East Germany in international diplomacy and trade.

These tense relations between the two countries started to thaw with the 'Ostpolitik' of West German Chancellor Willy Brandt. This new policy of 'open door' diplomacy resulted in West Germany finally recognizing the GDR with the Basic Treaty of 1972, which was signed in East Berlin on December 21st, 1972, and ratified the following year. West Germany agreed to cease calling itself the sole representative of the German people and the two countries agreed to exchange "permanent missions".

However, this designation meant that these established relations would stop short of 'full diplomatic recognition'. The Basic Treaty was a huge win for East Germany, which immediately attained official status with more Western countries and also benefited economically from the accord.

EUROPE: Norway and Denmark Vote on Joining the EEC

Der Bräutigam sagt nein   Zeichnung: Hartung

Voters in Norway and Denmark voted within a week of each other on whether or not to join what was then the European Economic Community (EEC), today the EU. The majority of Norwegians voted against membership on September 25th, 1972, with 53.5 per cent of voters opting to vote 'No'. Norwegian Prime Minister, Trygve Bratteli, who had campaigned hard for the country to join the EEC, resigned as a result of the defeat in the referendum. Norway's previous application to join the European economic federation had been blocked by France in 1962. A referendum on entry into what had become the European Union (EU) in 1994 was also rejected by Norwegian voters, that time by a larger margin than the 1972 referendum.

In Denmark, a referendum on joining the EEC was held on October 2nd, 1972, in which Danes voted to join the European bloc. The result of the vote was 63.3 percent in favour of joining, with an exceptionally high turnout of 90.1 percent. Denmark became a member of the EEC on January 1st, 1973, joining Ireland and the United Kingdom as members of the bloc on the same day. There had been a fierce, vocal opposition to joining the EEC within Denmark leading up to the referendum. Interestingly, at the time of the campaign for the 'Yes' vote, the then Danish Prime Minister, Jens Otto Krag, had vowed that Denmark would leave the EEC were the United Kingdom to ever leave.

UNITED STATES: Richard Nixon Wins Re-Election in a Landslide

On November 7th, U.S. President Richard Nixon defeated Senator George McGovern, the Democratic nominee from South Dakota in the 1972 Presidential election and was thus re-elected President of the United States. The election saw the lowest turnout since 1948, with only 55 percent of eligible voters bothering to vote. In a crushing victory, Nixon carried every single state in the Union except Massachusetts and was awarded an astounding 97 percent of the available electoral votes.

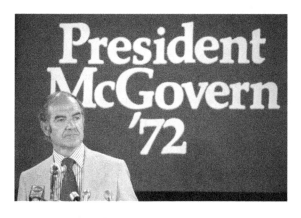

Nixon had been able to capitalize on a withdrawal from Vietnam based on "peace with honor," as well as relatively strong American economy. McGovern was considered an easy opponent for the hawkish Nixon, given that the Senator was an outspoken advocate for peace, especially in Vietnam. McGovern declared during his campaign that, "If I were President, it would take me twenty-four hours and the stroke of a pen to terminate all military operations in Southeast Asia." This was considered too extreme for many Americans, and he was even openly criticized, and his campaign actively derailed by many leading Democrats.

Interestingly, the Watergate scandal, which had begun to emerge earlier in 1972, had no impact on Nixon's electability. In fact, a poll taken on the eve of the election showed that the majority of Americans believed Nixon when he said he had nothing to do with the Watergate break-ins. By 1974, Nixon would resign due to Watergate - and bumper stickers would be made that read: "Don't blame me, I'm from Massachusetts!".

HUMAN INTEREST: The Uruguayan Rugby Team Crash in the Andes

Uruguayan Air Force flight 571 was an airplane charted by an Uruguayan amateur rugby team which crashed in the Andes Mountains in Argentina on October 13th, 1972. The Old Christians Club had chartered the plane to transport the team from Montevideo, Uruguay, to Santiago, Chile. On board were five crew members and 40 passengers, including rugby club members, friends and family. The flight had already been delayed due to poor weather in the mountains, forcing everyone to stay overnight in Mendoza, Argentina. The crash occurred at an altitude of approximately 3,500 meters or 11,500 feet in a remote valley in Argentina near the Chilean border.

Unfortunately, the last reported location of the aircraft was incorrect, which is a leading reason why initial rescue efforts were unsuccessful. The search was called off after eight days, although further search efforts were done by family members. Supplies on the plane consisted mainly of chocolate bars and wine, which quickly ran out. It was finally decided that the survivors resorted to cannibalism to survive. Of the 45 people aboard the plane,16 had died on impact and a further 13 died from their injuries or due to starvation.

After a few weeks, it was decided that two of the survivors set out on an arduous to get help. The two men eventually came across three herdsmen

in the village of Los
Maitenes in Chile and the
authorities were notified.
Due to bad weather, it
took two days for attempts
by helicopters to retrieve
all the survivors from the
wreck. The story was an
immediate international

sensation. In the end, only 16 people had survived the ordeal. The incident
became known as *El Milagro de los Andes* or the 'Miracle of the Andes'.

UGANDA: Idi Amin Expels Asians from Uganda

The dictator Idi Amin
seized control of Uganda
in 1971 after a military
coup that overthrew Milton
Obote as President. From
the outset, Amin was
obsessed with the Indian
minority that had lived in
Uganda since the 1800s and which had become an integral part of the
country's economy. Amin saw them as having too much control of the
country and wanted the country 'given back' to ethnic Africans. Amin
declared that a review of the citizenship status of Ugandan Asians be
undertaken. This escalated in August 1972, when Amin ordered the
expulsion of the Asian minority from Uganda. They were given 90 days
to leave the country.

This policy of targeting the Indian populations had already commenced with Obote during his first term as President of Uganda due to his policy of 'Africanization'. This led to the persecution of Indian 'traders' (the derogatory stereotype of Indians in the country at the time) by Obote's regime. The slang word for Indians as labourers, 'dukawallas,' became an anti-Indian slur with Amin in power.

Nearly all of the nearly 85,000 Indians in Uganda, fearing for their lives, chose to leave and emigrated to the United Kingdom, Canada, India, Kenya and other Commonwealth countries.

AUSTRALIA: Gough Whitlam Becomes First Labour Prime Minister Since 1949

The Labour Party, led by Gough Whitlam, beat the incumbent Liberal–Country coalition government, led by Prime Minister William McMahon, in the 1972 Australian federal election. The Labour Party's win was significant for two reasons: Firstly, it would be the first Labour

government since 1949, thereby ending 23 years of successive conservative Coalition governments. Secondly, the party's leader, Gough Whitlam was adamant that Australian forces be removed from the Vietnam War, a position which had been central to his platform throughout his election campaign. He had referred to the war as "disastrous and deluded," as well as violent and horrific for the Vietnamese people. He also stated that the war was against Australia's foreign policy interests.

Gough announced the formal withdrawal of Australian troops from Southeast-Asia within seven days of taking office, which came into effect on January 11th, 1973. The left-wing Whitlam Government would go on to implement a number of social programs,

including the institution of universal health care and free university education, the termination of compulsory military conscription and the roll-out of free legal aid.

JAPAN: Okinawa Returned to Japan

The United States finally returned the islands of Okinawa to Japan after having imposed American rule at the conclusion of World War II in 1945. A series of colorful ceremonies were held on May 15th, 1972, to commemorate the momentous hand-over. The event was also hailed as ushering in new phase of friendly relations between Japan and the United States on a more equal footing. The event was the culmination of the Okinawa Reversion Treaty (Agreement Between Japan and the United States of America Concerning the Ryukyu Islands and the Daito Islands) signed on June 17th, 1971, between Japan and the United States.

Vice President Spiro Agnew, who represented the U.S. at the ceremonies, stated that the hand-over would finally resolve the last major issue of the Pacific war between the U.S. and Japan, and which would undoubtedly create better ties between the two nations. The ceremonies were also attended by Emperor Hirohito and Empress Nagako, as well as other leading members of the Japanese government and military. The ceremonies were heavily guarded due to huge protests by Japanese citizens who were opposed to the continued presence of United States military bases on Okinawa.

SRI LANKA: Ceylon Becomes the Republic of Sri Lanka

On May 23rd, 1972, the former British colony of Ceylon became the socialist Republic of Sri Lanka. The country, which had first gained independence from

Britain in 1948, decided to change its name from Ceylon, which was derived from the Portuguese word given to the island. The name was considered outdated and colonialist. The name Sri Lanka was chosen, roughly translated from the Tamil and Sinhalese word 'Lanka,' meaning "great and beautiful island." The word 'Sri' was added for honorific purposes. The constitution for the newly formed independent country was also adopted that same day by its constituent assembly, as signed by Stanley Tillekerantne, the Speaker of the assembly.

Sirimavo Bandaranaike was inaugurated as the first Prime Minister of Sri Lanka. Mrs. Bandaranaike had previously become the world's first female head of government when she became Prime Minister of what was then the Dominion of Ceylon in 1960. In a speech that day, Mrs. Bandaranaike pledge the country's ongoing commitment to the non-alignment movement and dedication to the United Nations, although the country would continue to be known for a while as Ceylon at the UN and other international organizations. Sri Lanka would continue as a member of the British Commonwealth.

UNITED STATES: Governor George C Wallace Shot and Paralyzed

Governor George Wallace of Alabama was shot during an outdoor political rally on May 15th, 1972, in Laurel, Maryland. Wallace was running as a candidate for the 1972 Presidential election and was expected to do well in many of the Southern states. In fact, the very next day Wallace won major victories in the primaries of Michigan and Maryland. Three others at the rally also had gunshot wounds. They had all been shot by 21-year-old Arthur Bremer with a .38 revolver. Bremer had originally wanted to shoot President Richard Nixon, but decided that Wallace would be an easier target instead.

A few weeks later, Shirley Chisholm, who was the first black woman elected to Congress and one of Wallace's opponents for the Democratic presidential nomination, famously paid Wallace a visit in hospital. The visit was highly symbolic, given that Wallace was a known segregationist who had previously run for office with decidedly racist campaigns, although his 1972 run was more moderate. Wallace, now paralyzed from the waist down, remained in hospital for several months and was forced

to end his presidential campaign. Wallace would go on to have a dramatic change of political opinion in the 1980s, becoming a firm advocate of civil rights and highly popular in the African American community.

CHESS: Chess Matches Between Boris Spassky and Bobby Fischer in Iceland

A series of chess matches between legendary chess masters Bobby Fischer of the U.S. and the Soviet Union's Boris Spassky are still considered the most exciting chess world championships of all time. The championship took place between July 11th and August 31st, 1972,

in Reykjavik, Iceland. The mercurial and often temperamental Fischer had threatened to not even attend the series in Iceland, which resulted in U.S. Secretary of State Henry Kissinger phoning Fischer and begging him to do so.

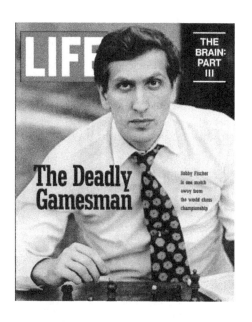

During the championship, Fischer made accusations of there being various ploys used by his opponent's 'handlers' to make him lose, from cameras that made a 'buzzing' sound (that no one else heard) to even electronic bugging devices. Fischer would eventually come from behind to win the championship by 12½ point to Spassky's 8½ points, becoming the first-ever American champion. Fischer's triumph ended a run of 10 consecutive Soviet wins and broke the 24-year stronghold by the Soviet Chess School on world chess. The 1984 album and hit 1986 West End musical *Chess* was loosely based on the 1972 championship between Fischer and Spassky.

LAW ENFORCEMENT: First Female Agents of the FBI

Founder and former Director of the FBI Director, J. Edgar Hoover had a strict rile that only men could be special agents in the FBI. That rule had changed shortly after his death in May 1972 when FBI Acting Director L. Patrick Gray announced that women applicants would now be considered for special agent training. However, it was stressed that all the existing requirements for FBI special agents would remain unchanged during the intense 14-week training course, including the expert use of firearms such as a .38 caliber revolver, shotgun and rifle, as well as the program's grueling physical fitness program.

Joanne Pierce Misko and Susan Roley Malone became the first women to be allowed to join the Federal Bureau of Investigation (FBI) when they joined their 43 male counterparts at the FBI's Special Agent training course in Quantico, Virginia, in July 1972. Joanne Misko had been a nun in New York for 10 years before commencing at the FBI in 1970 as a researcher. She was 31 years old when she commenced her FBI training. Susan Malone, who was 25 when she started her training, had already made her mark as a U.S. Marine, and decided to apply for the FBI when encouraged to do so by

her friends. The two women would live together, work out together and would become lifelong friends. Malone would later say that the two women quickly proved their worth with the other trainees. She said: "We wanted to be agents first. We just happened to be women."

OLYMPIC GAMES: Mark Spitz Makes a Splash

Fortunately, there was joy at the 1972 Summer Olympics in Munich. The American swimmer Mark Spitz would win a stunning seven gold medals at the 1972 Games. He won gold in every event he entered and did so in just eight days. Equally remarkably, Spitz also achieved new world records in six of the seven events in which he won the gold medal. Spitz won his gold medals in the following events and in the following order:

* 200-meters butterfly
* 4 x 100-meters freestyle relay
* 200-meters freestyle
* 100-meters butterfly
* 4 x 200-meters freestyle relay
* 100-meters freestyle
* 4 x 100-meters medley relay

His teammates hoisted Spitz onto their shoulders and took him on a victory lap around the pool after he'd won his seventh gold in the 4x100 meters

31

medley relay. No other athlete had won that number of gold medals at a single Olympiad, a record that would only be broken when another American swimmer, Michael Phelps, won eight gold medals at the 2008 Beijing Olympics.

AUTOMOBILES: Volkswagen Beetle Becomes Most-Sold Car in History

On February 17th, 1972, the 15,007,034th Volkswagen Beetle rolled off the assembly line, breaking the world record for production of a car model. Until then, the record had been held for more than four decades by the Ford Motor Company's iconic Model T, which was in production from 1908 and 1927. The Volkswagen Beetle had dated back to 1930s Germany and had been designed by famous Austrian engineer Ferdinand Porsche. His mandate was to build an inexpensive, mass-produced "people's car" or Volkswagen, as it was named in German.

Reliability, great road-handling and inexpensive maintenance costs had all contributed to the immense and enduring success of the VW Beetle. It became a fixture in global pop culture, including being an integral part

of the 'Flower Child' era of the 1960s and as the main 'character' in the highly successful *Herbie* movies, which featured a 1963 Beetle. The Volkswagen Beetle would go on to have over 21 million units produced. The last original Beetle would roll off the production line in Puebla, Mexico, on July 30th, 2003.

GAMES: Magnavox Odyssey and Pong Video Games Both Released

Magnavox released its Magnavox Odyssey in early 1972, making it the first home video game system ever released. It would usher in the advent of game consoles and home video gaming. The Odyssey set consisted of a white, black, and brown box that connected to a television set, with two rectangular controllers attached by wires that could be used by opposing players. Additional games and accessories, like a light-gun, as well as dice, decks of cards, play money and poker chips, were sold separately for the game. All these accessories were included to make the video game feel more like the board games that were very popular at the time. Approximately 350,000 units of Magnovox Odyssey were sold.

Also released in 1972, Atari's Pong video game was a runaway success and far more popular than the Magnavox Odyssey. Pong was a simple video game akin to tennis, in that it featured two paddles and a ball, with a point awarded each time an opponent missed a ball. The winner would be the first one to get 10 points. The game had simple sound

effects and was considered fairly basic even at the time, but its popularity took off with youngsters who played it in arcades. By 1973, the arcade version was being shipped all over the world. Pong had its initial huge success with its arcade version, with a later home version of the game released in 1975. Atari was founded by Nolan Bushnell in 1972 in order to create video games and would go on to be a market leader during the 1980s.

Other Notable Events of 1972

UNITED NATIONS:

UNESCO launched the 'World Heritage Site' program at a conference in Paris, France, on November 16th, 1972, as signed by 196 countries and territories. The Convention Concerning the Protection of the World Cultural and Natural Heritage focuses on the preservation of places around the world of cultural significance and the conservation of unique or fragile natural environments and ecosystems. The Convention defines the kind of Natural or cultural sites of distinction have been considered since then on the prestigious World Heritage List.

SPACE EXPLORATION: President Richard Nixon announced on January 5th, 1972, that NASA would proceed with the development of a reusable low-cost space shuttle system. NASA would announce on March 15th that the proposed shuttle would use two solid propellant rocket motors. The first shuttle mission with crew on board, *Columbia*, took off into space on April 12th, 1981.

TECHNOLOGY: The world's first hand-held scientific calculator, the HP-35 Scientific Calculator, was released by Hewlett-Packard in 1972. It was called the HP-35 because it had 35 keys. It was considered a major milestone in that it quickly replaced the slide rule that had been used by generations of engineers and scientists for rapid calculations. It was immensely popular, selling 100,000 units within months of launch.

CRIME: The hotel robbery that took place on January 2nd, 1972, at The Pierre Hotel in New York City was worth $3 million (approximately $27 million today). The robbery took under three hours before the

morning shift began at the hotel, during which time close to one quarter of the 208 lock boxes in the hotel vault were breached and their valuables stolen. The Pierre Hotel robbery would later be listed in the Guinness Book of World Records as the largest, most successful hotel robbery in history.

AVIATION: Vesna Vulovic, a Yugoslav air stewardess, was the sole survivor of a suspected bomb that tore apart a Yugoslav Airlines Douglas DC-9 over Czechoslovakia on January

26th, 1972. Vulovic miraculously survived falling from the aircraft from a height of 33,000 feet (10,000 meters). It is believed that Vulovic was saved due to being trapped by a food cart in the plane's tail section as it plummeted down to earth. She was rescued when a woodsman heard her screams amid the fallen debris. Although paralyzed at first, she soon regained all mobility and returned to work at a desk job at the Yugoslav airline. She was later entered into the Guinness Book of World Records for surviving the highest fall ever by a person without a parachute.

CRIME: Clifford Irving was revealed as being 'the great impostor,' after it was found that his alleged book done with the blessing and input of hyper-secretive billionaire, Howard Hughes, was a giant hoax. It had all

started in 1971 when Irving convinced McGraw-Hill, a well-respected New York City book publishing house, that he had secured the rights from the reclusive Hughes to write his autobiography. He was paid a $765,000 advance (approximately $4.8 million in today's money) to complete the book. It was eventually found by Swiss authorities that the account for "Helga R. Hughes" into which monies had been paid for the book was in fact held by Irving's wife. Irving was sentenced to 2½ years in prison in June 1972 and also made to pay back all the money he'd defrauded from McGraw-Hill.

SPORTS: 1972 Winter Olympics - Sapporo, Japan

The 1972 Winter Olympic Games was held from February 3rd to February 13th, 1972, in Sapporo, Hokkaidō, Japan. The Games in Sapporo were the first Winter Olympic Games that took place outside Europe and North America. There was controversy even before the Games commenced over the issue of amateurism. According to Olympic rules at the time, only amateur athletes could take part in an Olympiad.

As such, Austrian skier Karl Schranz was declared ineligible for the Sapporo Games because his name and photo had been used with his consent for commercial advertising. Yet fully professional ice hockey players from communist countries were allowed to compete as they were considered 'amateurs' by their home associations.

Thirty-five nations participated in the Games and the Soviet Union won the most number of gold medals (8) and total medals (16), with East Germany placing second for both. Switzerland placed third overall in medals and 11 countries won medals across 35 events contested in six different sports.

Notable achievements at the 1972 Winter Olympics included:
- Galina Kulakova of the USSR won all three cross-country skiing events for women - the 5km and 10km individual events and as the anchor for the Soviet Union's relay team.
- Ard Schenk of the Netherland won three gold medals in speed skating (1500m, 5000m and 10000m events) - he was so popular in the Netherlands that a flower was named in his honor: *Crocus chrysanthus Ard Schenk*.
- Yukio Kasaya won in ski-jumping, making it the first gold medal ever won by Japan at a Winter Olympics - Kasaya would go on to

be Japan's flag bearer at the opening ceremonies of the 1976 and 1998 Winter Olympics.

➢ Francisco 'Paquito' Fernández Ochoa won the men's slalom skiing event by a full second and became the first-ever gold medal winner for Spain at an Olympic Winter Games - many have considered this the most surprising winner of the entire Games at Sapporo.

SPORTS: Winners of Major Sporting Competitions in 1972

American Football:
Super Bowl VI: Dallas Cowboys [beat the Miami Dolphins]

Association Football:
UEFA European Championship [hosted in Belgium]: West Germany [beat the USSR in the final]
European Cup Winner's Cup: Rangers F.C., Scotland [beat Dinamo Moscow in the final]

English FA Cup: Leeds United [beat Arsenal in the final]
English First Division: Derby County
German Bundesliga: Bayern München
Italian Serie A: Juventus
Spanish La Liga: Real Madrid

Baseball:

World Series: Oakland Athletics [beat the Cincinnati Reds]

Basketball:

NBA Finals: Los Angeles Lakers [beat the New York Knicks]

Cycling:

Tour de France: Eddy Merckx, Belgium

Formula One:

World Champion: Emerson Fittipaldi, Brazil [also most wins: 5]
Winning Constructor: Lotus-Ford

Golf:

Masters Tournament: Jack Nicklaus

U.S. Open: Jack Nicklaus

British Open: Lee Trevino

Ice Hockey:

Stanley Cup: Boston Bruins [beat the New York Rangers]

BOSTON BRUINS
STANLEY CUP CHAMPIONS 1971-72

1ˢᵗ Row Gerry Cheevers Johnny Bucyk Phil Esposito Milt Schmidt Tom Johnson Ed Westfall Ted Green Ed Johnson
2ⁿᵈ Row D.Canny Mike Walton Garnet Bailey Carol Vadnais Don Awrey Don Marcotte Wayne Cashman J.Foristal
3ʳᵈ Row Johnny McKenzie Bobby Orr Dallas Smith Ken Hodge Derek Sanderson Fred Stanfield

Tennis:

Men's and Women's winners for the four Grand Slam events:

Australian Open: Ken Rosewall, Australia | Virginia Wade, UK

French Open: Andrés Gimeno, Spain | Billie Jean King, USA

Wimbledon: Stan Smith, USA | Billie Jean King, USA

US Open: Ilie Năstase, Romania Billie Jean King*, USA

Davis Cup: United States [beat Romania]

* *Billie Jean King became the first tennis player in the Open era to win a repeat singles Grand Slam event.*

Associated Press Male Athlete of the Year – Mark Spitz, USA - Swimming

Associated Press Female Athlete of the Year – Olga Korbut, USSR - Gymnastics

MOVIES: Top 20 Highest-Grossing Films of 1972

1972 was considered an exceptional year in film, both critically and commercially. These were the Top 20 highest-grossing movies of 1972:

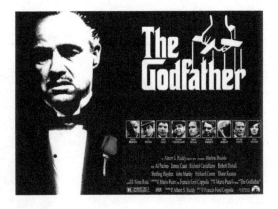

Rank	Movie	Genre	1972 Gross	Total Tickets Sold
1	The Godfather	Drama	$133,744,459	78,673,211
2	The Poseidon Adventure	Action	$93,300,000	54,882,352
3	What's Up, Doc?	Comedy	$57,142,740	33,613,376
4	Deliverance	Thriller	$46,122,355	27,130,797
5	Deep Throat	Adult/Porn	$45,000,000	26,470,588
6	Jeremiah Johnson	Western	$44,693,786	26,290,462
7	Cabaret	Musical	$41,326,446	24,309,674
8	The Getaway	Action	$36,734,619	21,608,599
9	Last Tango in Paris	Drama	$36,144,824	21,261,661
10	Lady Sings the Blues	Drama	$19,726,490	11,603,817
11	Everything You Always Wanted To Know About Sex But Were Too Afraid To Ask	Comedy	$18,016,290	10,597,817
12	The Valachi Papers	Crime	$17,106,087	10,062,404
13	Sounder	Drama	$16,889,761	9,935,153
14	The Life and Times of Judge Roy Bean	Western	$16,530,578	9,723,869
15	Pete 'n' Tillie	Comedy	$14,999,969	8,823,511
16	Frenzy	Thriller	$12,600,000	7,411,764
17	Across 110th Street	Thriller	$10,000,000	5,882,352
18	Shaft's Big Score	Action	$10,000,000	5,882,352

Rank	Movie	Genre	1972 Gross	Total Tickets Sold
19	Conquest of the Planet of the Apes	Action	$9,700,000	5,705,882
20	The Cowboys	Western	$7,500,000	4,411,764

Total U.S. Gross of All Movies: $696,708,404
Total Tickets Sold in U.S.: $409,828,463

Of note from the above table is how *The Godfather* made $40 million more in box office earnings than the second highest-grossing film of 1972, *The Poseidon Adventure*. Its ticket sales also meant that more than one in every six movie tickets sold in the U.S. in 1972 were for *The Godfather*. When adjusted for inflation, the $133,744,000 earned by The Godfather means it would have earned more than 840 million in today's money. Also notable is the fact that an X-rated porn film, *Deep Throat*, and an X-rated sexual drama, *Last Tango in Paris*, also made it into the Top 10 highest-grossing films of the year.

MOVIES: The Stunning Success of *The Godfather*

The enormous success of Francis Ford Coppola's sprawling and epic Mob drama *The Godfather*, which became the biggest-grossing film of 1972 and a cultural phenomenon, was not remotely expected. In fact,

expectations at Paramount Pictures were quite low for the film, even though the 1969 book by Mario Puzo, from which the film was adapted, was a best-seller hit. However, not only had Coppola directed a string of box office duds, but Marlon Brando, the central character and main draw of the film, was deemed as a 'has been' by the movie industry. Also, Puzo's book had been dismissed by most critics as pulp fiction and hardly the stuff of serious drama.

Even more 'damning' for the move was that it had a cast principally composed of relative unknowns and B-grade players such as Al Pacino, James Caan and Diane Keaton. Coppola had even cast his sister, Talia Shire, in a central role, which many also felt was further evidence of a film that was bound to flop. However, the film was hailed as a masterpiece on the day of its premiere, March 24th, 1972, and would go on to win three Oscars at the Academy Awards the next year, including Best Picture.

For many film critics and pundits, *The Godfather* changed American cinema forever, with its dark, violent themes told with epic, beautifully rendered artistry never before seen in the genre. It also shed a sinister light on the so-called 'American Dream.' Since then, *The Godfather* appears consistently on the lists of best American films of all time, often coming second only to Orson Welles' classic, *Citizen Kane*, as it does for the prestigious American Film Institute (AFI).

MOVIES: The Arthouse Sensation: *Last Tango in Paris*

If *The Godfather* was the commercial success story of 1972, then Bernardo Bertolucci's erotic drama, *Last Tango in Paris*, was the arthouse hit of the year. The film caused much controversy due to its raw portrayal of sexual violence and emotional turmoil. It immediately got an X rating by the Motion Picture Association of America (MPAA) upon its release in the United States.

The film's release in France caused two-hour queues during its first run at the seven cinemas that screened the film. It was even reported that thousands of Spaniards travelled hundreds of miles to see the film at French cinemas in Biarritz and Perpignan, since the film was banned in Franco's fascist Spain. The film initially grossed an unprecedented $100,000 in six days when released in Italy. However, soon all copies of the film were seized by the police and Bertolucci, an Italian, would later be charged for alleged "obscenity". Four years later in 1976, the Italian Supreme Court would order all copies of the film in Italy to be destroyed and Bertolucci was served with a four-month suspended prison sentence, with all his civil rights revoked for five years.

MOVIES: A Hit Adult Animated Film Called *Fritz the Cat*

Fritz the Cat was an adult animated black comedy written and directed by Ralph Bakshi and based on the comic strip by legendary cartoonist, Robert Crumb. The film focused on Fritz, a womanizing, fraudster cat who lives in an animal version of New York City during the mid-to-late 1960s. The film was a scathing satire focused on American counterculture, including the free love movement and political activist hacks, as well as race relations and the cultural mores of the time. It also featured sex and violence never seen before in a mass-released animated movie.

Produced on a small budget of $700,000, it was a breakthrough in that an adult-themed animated film was considered off-limits in that animation was very much seen as a children's genre. Pundits believed the film was further doomed when it was slapped with an X rating by the MPAA. There was also a common misunderstanding among many Americans that Fritz the Cat was a porn movie, which it was not. The film quickly gained momentum after getting rave reviews from *Rolling Stone* magazine and *The New York Times* and was even accepted to play at the Cannes Film Festival. It became a commercial hit and quickly attained cult status. It is often accredited with being the film that broke the barrier for adult-themed animated films.

MOVIES: Other Arthouse and Critical Hits of 1972

One of the most successful and critically acclaimed arthouse films of the year was *The Discreet Charm of the Bourgeoisie,* a surrealist farce by another legendary director, Spain's Luis Buñuel. The film focused on a group of well-heeled friends whose dinner plans are usurped by a series of off-beat occurrences. It starred some of Europe's biggest names in cinema at the time, including Spain's Fernando Rey and France's Stéphane Audran, Jean-Pierre Cassel and Michel Piccoli. The film would go on to win the Academy Award for Best Foreign Language Film in 1973.

Another successful arthouse film in 1972 was *Aguirre, the Wrath of God,* an epic historical drama produced, written and directed by German director, Werner Herzog. Like others of Herzog's films, it quickly became an international cult favorite. One of the most critically acclaimed Russian directors of all time, Andrei Tarkovsky, released *Solaris* in 1972 to generally excellent reviews. The film is often cited as one of the greatest science fiction films ever made.

Tarkovsky would later further develop ideas from this film into another classic film of his, 1979's *Stalker*. Other well-received foreign-language films of the year included *Roma* by Italian maestro Federico Fellini, *State of Siege* by French-based Greek director, Costa-Gavras, and *The New Land* by Sweden's Jan Troell.

Smaller English-language films that were critically acclaimed too included *The Effect of Gamma Rays on Man-in-the-Moon Marigolds*, directed by Hollywood actor Paul Newman, *Butterflies are Free*, starring Goldie Hawn and Edward Albert, and *Sleuth*, based on the hit play and starring Laurence Oliver and Michael Caine.

MOVIES: Major Film Awards of 1972

Academy Awards:

The 44th annual Academy Awards were held at the Dorothy Chandler Pavilion in Los Angeles on April 10th, 1972. The principal winners were:

Best Picture: *The French Connection**

Best Director: William Friedkin for *The French Connection**

Best Actress: Jane Fonda *Klute**

Best Actor: Gene Hackman for *The French Connection**

Best Supporting Actor: Ben Johnson for *The Last Picture Show**

Best Supporting Actress: Cloris Leachman for *The Last Picture Show*

Best Foreign Language Film: *The Garden of the Finzi-Continis*, directed by Vittorio de Sica, Italy

* *These films / performances also won the Golden Globe in 1972 for their respective categories.*

Honorary Oscar: Charlie Chaplin - *for "the incalculable effect he has had in making motion pictures the art form of this century".*

Chaplin, who had never won a competitive Oscar during his career to that point, received a 12-minute standing ovation, the longest in the history of the Academy Awards.

Cannes Film Festival:

Palme d'Or: [tie]

The Working Class Goes to Heaven, directed by Elio Petri, Italy

The Mattei Affair, directed by Francesco Rosi, Italy

Grand Prix Spécial du Jury: *Solaris*, directed by Andrei Tarkovsky, USSR

Best Director: Miklós Jancsó for *Red Psalm*

Best Actress: Susannah York for *Images*

Best Actor: Jean Yanne for *We Won't Grow Old Together*

Jury Prize: *Slaughterhouse-Five*, directed by George Roy Hill

Berlin Film Festival:

Golden Bear: *The Canterbury Tales*, directed by Pier Paolo Pasolini, Italy / France

Venice Film Festival:

Best Foreign Film: A Clockwork Orange, directed by Stanley Kubrick, USA

MUSIC: Top Songs and Albums of 1972 - USA, UK & International

The following were the Top 30 songs in the United States in 1972, according to *Billboard*:

Rank	Artist	Music
1	Don McLean	American Pie
2	Hot Butter	Popcorn
3	Harry Nilsson	Without You
4	The Moody Blues	Nights in White Satin
5	Neil Young	Heart of Gold
6	Roberta Flack	The First Time Ever I Saw Your Face
7	Daniel Boone	Beautiful Sunday
8	Al Green	Let's Stay Together
9	Gilbert O'Sullivan	Alone Again (Naturally)

Rank	Artist	Music
10	Gilbert O'Sullivan	Clair
11	Dr Hook	Sylvia's Mother
12	Melanie	Brand New Key
13	Neil Diamond	Song Sung Blue
14	Derek & The Dominos	Layla
15	America	Horse With No Name
16	The Temptations	Papa Was a Rolling Stone
17	Mouth & MacNeal	How Do You Do!
18	Johnny Nash	I Can See Clearly Now
19	Donny Osmond	Puppy Love
20	The Sweet	Little Willy
21	The New Seekers	I'd Like to Teach the World to Sing
22	The Hollies	Long Cool Woman in a Black Dress
23	The Royal Scots Dragoon Guards	Amazing Grace
24	Michael Jackson	Ben
25	Bill Withers	Lean On Me
26	Alice Cooper	School's Out
27	Middle of The Road	Sacramento (A Wonderful Town)
28	Gary Glitter	Rock 'n' Roll (Part 2)
29	The Osmonds	Crazy Horses
30	Elton John	Rocket Man

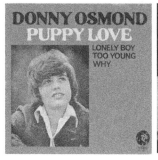  

These were the Top 20 songs of 1972 according to their worldwide sales:

Rank	Artist	Music
1	Don McLean	American Pie
2	Harry Nilsson	Without You
3	Hot Butter	Popcorn
4	Daniel Boone	Beautiful Sunday
5	Neil Young	Heart of Gold
6	The Moody Blues	Nights in White Satin
7	Roberta Flack	The First Time Ever I Saw Your Face
8	Al Green	Let's Stay Together
9	Donny Osmond	Puppy Love
10	Gilbert O'Sullivan	Alone Again (Naturally)
11	Gilbert O'Sullivan	Clair
12	America	Horse With No Name
13	Melanie	Brand New Key
14	Derek & The Dominos	Layla
15	Dr Hook	Sylvia's Mother
16	Johnny Nash	I Can See Clearly Now
17	Derek & The Dominos	Layla
18	The Royal Scots Dragoon Guards	Amazing Grace
19	The Temptations	Papa Was a Rolling Stone
20	The Hollies	Long Cool Woman in a Black Dress

And these were the Top 20 albums of 1972 in worldwide sales:

Rank	Artist	Album
1	Neil Young	Harvest
2	The Rolling Stones	Exile On Main Street
3	Deep Purple	Machine Head
4	David Bowie	Ziggy Stardust & The Spiders From Mars
5	Simon & Garfunkel	Simon & Garfunkel's Greatest Hits
6	Don McLean	American Pie
7	Jethro Tull	Thick As A Brick
8	Cat Stevens	Catch Bull At Four
9	Paul Simon	Paul Simon
10	Elton John	Honky Chateau
11	Stevie Wonder	Talking Book
12	The Moody Blues	Seventh Sojourn

Rank	Artist	Album
13	George Harrison & Various Artists	Concert For Bangladesh
14	Rod Stewart	Never A Dull Moment
15	Chicago	Chicago V
16	Curtis Mayfield	Superfly
17	America	America
18	Alice Cooper	School's Out
19	Yes	Close To The Edge
20	Roberta Flack	First Take

These were the Top 20 Hits of 1972 on the UK charts:

Rank	Artist	Hit
1	Nilsson	Without You
2	Pipes & Drums & The Military Band Of The Royal Scots Dragoon Guard	Amazing Grace
3	Donny Osmond	Puppy Love
4	The New Seekers	I'd Like To Teach The World To Sing (In Perfect Harmony)
5	Lieutenant Pigeon	Mouldy Old Dough
6	Chuck Berry	My Ding-A-Ling
7	T Rex	Metal Guru

Rank	Artist	Hit
8	Neil Reid	Mother Of Mine
9	Chicory Tip	Son Of My Father
10	Don McLean	American Pie
11	Don McLean	Vincent
12	Alice Cooper	School's Out
13	Gary Glitter	Rock And Roll Parts 1 And 2
14	The New Seekers	Beg, Steal Or Borrow
15	Slade	Mama Weer All Crazee Now
16	Rod Stewart	You Wear It Well
17	Gilbert O'Sullivan	Clair
18	T Rex	Telegram Sam
19	Faron Young	It's Four In The Morning
20	Slade	Take Me Bak 'Ome

MUSIC: Grammy Award Winners

The 14th annual Grammy Awards were held at the Felt Forum in New York City on March 14th, 1972, and hosted by Andy Williams. Some of the principal winners were:

Record of the Year: Lou Adler (producer) & Carole King for *It's Too Late*

Album of the Year: Lou Adler (producer) & Carole King for *Tapestry*
Song of the Year: Carole King (songwriter) for *You've Got a Friend*
Best New Artist: Carly Simon

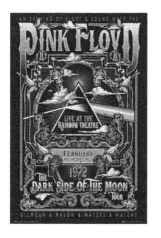 

MUSIC: Eurovision Song Contest

The 17th annual Eurovision Song Contest was held in Edinburgh,
Scotland, on March 25th, 1972, and was hosted by Scottish-born
Hollywood actress, Moira Shearer. Eighteen countries participated in
the contest and no country received the dreaded 'nul' or zero points this
year! The top 3 results were:

WINNER: *Après toi* by Vicky
Leandros (Luxembourg) - 128 points
2nd: *Beg, Steal or Borrow* by The
New Seekers (United Kingdom) -
114 points
3rd: *Nur die Liebe läßt uns leben* by
Mary Roos (Germany) - 107 points

The winner, Vicky Leandros, had competed before for Luxembourg at the 1967 Eurovision Song Contest, where she placed fourth. Her winning song, *Après toi*, including its English version called *Come What May*, went on to be a huge international hit, getting to Number 1 on the hit parades of Belgium, France, the Netherlands, South Africa and Switzerland. It remains one of the most commercially successful Eurovision winners to date, after *Waterloo* by Sweden's ABBA (1974 winner and Number 1 in 11 countries worldwide) and *Puppet on a String* by the UK's Sandie Shaw (1967 winner and with 10 Number 1s worldwide).

TELEVISION: Two New Hit Comedy Series on U.S. Television

M*A*S*H* (an acronym for Mobile Army Surgical Hospital) first aired on September 17th, 1972, and was a comedy series based on the 1970 critically-acclaimed, Oscar-nominated film of the same name, directed by Robert Altman. The cast for the 1972 season was led by Alan Alda as Hawkeye Pierce and Wayne Rogers as Trapper John McIntyre. *M*A*S*H* ran from 1972 to 1983, which was more than three times as long as the Korean War that was its setting. It was ranked #25 in TV Guide's *50 Greatest TV Shows of All Time.* The series was immensely popular during its run, culminating with its final episode in 1983, which was the most-watched finale in U.S. television history.

Maude first aired on September 12th, 1972, starring Bea Arthur as Maude Findlay, an outspoken, politically liberal woman living in suburban Westchester County, New York, with Bill Macy playing Walter Findlay, Maude's fourth and often hen-pecked husband. The show became famous for broaching many of the leading social issues of the day, particularly women's rights and racial equality. It ran for seven seasons. *Maude* ran for seven seasons and was the first spin-off series of the highly popular comedy series, *All in the Family*, which in 1972 was the Number 1 show on U.S. television (see below).

TELEVISION: The Biggest TV Series / Specials / Shows in the US and UK During 1972

Below were the Top 20 TV shows on U.S. televisions during 1972:

Rank	Show	Network	Share Rating
1	All in the Family	CBS	34.0
2	The Flip Wilson Show	NBC	28.2
3	Marcus Welby, M.D.	ABC	27.8
4	Gunsmoke	CBS	26.0
5	ABC Movie of the Week	ABC	25.6
6	Sanford and Son	NBC	25.2
7	Mannix	CBS	24.8
8	Funny Face	CBS	23.9
9	Adam-12	NBC	23.8
10	The Mary Tyler Moore Show	CBS	23.7
11	Here's Lucy	CBS	23.6
12	Hawaii Five-O	CBS	23.6
13	Medical Center	CBS	23.5
14	The NBC Mystery Movie	NBC	23.2
15	Ironside	NBC	23.0
16	The Partridge Family	ABC	22.6
17	The F.B.I.	ABC	22.4
18	The New Dick Van Dyke Show	CBS	22.2

Rank	Show	Network	Share Rating
19	The Wonderful World of Disney	NBC	22.0
20	Bonanza	NBC	21.9

TELEVISION: Emmy Award Winners

The 24th annual Grammy Awards were held at the Hollywood Palladium in Los Angeles on May 14th, 1972, and hosted by Johnny Carson. Some of the principal winners were:

Outstanding Drama Series: *Elizabeth R*

Outstanding Comedy Series: *All in the Family*

Outstanding Variety Series - Musical: *The Carol Burnett Show*

Outstanding Variety Series - Talk: *The Dick Cavett Show*

Outstanding Daytime Drama: *The Doctors*

Outstanding Children's Programming: *Sesame Street*

Most Wins: *All in the Family* - 6

Dick Cavett, who couldn't care less about clothes

Below were the Top 20 TV Shows or TV specials in the UK during 1972:

Rank	Show	Network
1	Eurovision Song Contest	BBC
2	This is Your Life	ITV
3	Miss World 1972	BBC
4	Steptoe and Son	BBC
5	Love Thy Neighbor	ITV
6	Till Death Do Us Part	BBC
7	Coronation Street	ITV
8	A Family at War	ITV
9	Public Eye	ITV
10	Opportunity Knocks	ITV
11	Benny Hill Show	ITV
12	On the Buses	ITV
13	The Strauss Family	ITV
14	Suspicion	ITV
15	Bless This House	ITV
16	News at Ten	ITV
17	The Persuaders	ITV
18	Football: England v West Germany	ITV
19	Nine O'Clock News	BBC
20	Carry On Christmas	ITV

FASHION: Ready-To-Wear and Haute Couture of 1972

PEOPLE: Famous & Accomplished People Born in 1972

These were the famous and accomplished people who were born in 1972:

January 1 - Catherine McCormack, English actress

January 5 - Sakis Rouvas, Greek singer and actor

January 11 - Amanda Peet, American actress

January 22 - Gabriel Macht, American actor

January 23 - Ewen Bremner, Scottish actor

January 28 - Amy Coney-Barrett, American lawyer and Supreme Court Justice

February 11 - Kelly Slater, American surfer

February 14 - Rob Thomas, American singer and songwriter

February 14 - Najwa Nimri, Spanish actress and singer

February 29 - Pedro Sánchez, Spanish politician and Prime Minister

March 6 - Shaquille O'Neal, American basketball player

March 13 – Common, American actor and singer

March 18 – Dane Cook, American comedian

March 23 – Judith Godrèche, French actress

March 26 – Leslie Mann, American actress

March 28 – Nick Frost, English actor, comedian, writer and producer

March 31 – Alejandro Amenábar, Spanish director, writer and soundtrack composer

April 15 - Trine Dyrholm, Danish actress

April 16 - Tracy K. Smith, American Poet Laureate

April 17 – Jennifer Garner, American actress

April 20 - Carmen Electra, American actress and model

May 2 – Dwayne Johnson aka 'The Rock,' American actor

May 7 - Asghar Farhadi, Iranian director and writer

May 20 - Busta Rhymes, American rapper and songwriter

May 25 - Octavia Spencer, American actress

May 28 – Chiara Mastroianni, French actress

May 28 - Roland Møller, Danish actor

May 29 - Laverne Cox, American actress, producer and activist

June 2 - Wayne Brady, American actor, comedian and presenter

June 2 - Wentworth Miller, American actor

June 7 – Karl Urban, New Zealand actor

June 16 - John Cho, South Korean American actor

June 19 - Jean Dujardin, French actor

June 19 - Robin Tunney, American actress

June 23 – Selma Blair, American actress

June 23 - Zinedine Zidane, French football player

June 28 – Alessandro Nivola, American actor

July 5 – Gilles Lellouche, French actor and director

July 10 - Sofia Vergara, Colombian American actress, presenter and model

July 23 - Marlon Wayans, American comedian, actor and writer

July 27 – Maya Rudolph, American actress and comedian

July 28 – Elizabeth Berkley, American actress

July 29 – Wil Wheaton, American actor
August 15 – Ben Affleck, American actor, director and writer
August 30 – Cameron Diaz, American actress
September 6 - Idris Elba, English actor
September 9 – Goran Visnjic, Croatian-American actor
September 15 - Jimmy Carr, English comedian, writer and TV host

September 21 - Liam Gallagher, English rock singer
September 27 – Gwyneth Paltrow, American actress
September 28 - Dita von Teese, American cabaret artiste and actress
October 5 - Tom Hooper, English director and producer

October 17 – Eminem, American rapper and actor
October 22 – Saffron Burrows, English American actress
October 29 - Gabrielle Union, American actress, voice artist and author

November 1 - Toni Collette, Australian actress
November 1 – Jenny McCarthy, American actress
November 4 - Luís Figo, Portuguese football player

November 6 - Thandiwe Newton, English actress

November 6 - Rebecca Romijn, American actress

November 7 – Jeremy and Jason London, American actors

November 8 - Gretchen Mol, American actress

November 9 - Eric Dane, American actor

November 14 – Josh Duhamel, American actor

November 15 - Jonny Lee Miller, English actor

November 26 – Arjun Rampal, Indian actor

December 14 - Miranda Hart, English comedienne and actress

December 15 – Stuart Townsend, Irish actor

December 19 – Alyssa Milano, American actress

December 22 - Vanessa Paradis, French actress and singer

December 29 – Jude Law, English actor

STATISTICS: 1972 in Numbers

The following were some of the leading census and other important statistics for the United States in 1972:

Population: 209,896,021

Life expectancy: 71.2 years

Federal spending: $230.68 billion

Federal debt: $435.9 billion

Inflation: 4.3%

Consumer Price Index: 41.8

Unemployment: 5.9%

Dow-Jones

High: 1036

Low: 921

Gold price (high): $70.00

Silver price (high): $2.03

These were the median U.S. prices for selected products and assets in 1972:

Median household income: $9,697.00

New home: $30,500.00 [by way of comparison, a split-level home in an upper-middle suburb with a living room, dining room, 3 bedrooms, 3 bathrooms, central air conditioning, a double garage and cathedral ceilings in Iowa City would have cost $32,400]

New car: $2,078 (Ford Pinto) | $2,796 (Plymouth Fury)

Used car: $1,395 (1967 Mustang GT V8) | $100 (1963 Chevrolet Impala)

Average monthly rent: $165.00

Gallon of regular gas: $0.36

Median salaries by profession or job title:

Presenting Datsun 610.
Considering the luxury,
its economy is all the more remarkable.

Own a Datsun Original.

Chartered accountant: $15.000/year

Electrician (starting): $7.800/year

Insurance underwriter: $12.500/year

Medical sales rep: $9.500/year + car

Telephone operator: $101/week

Typist: $120/week

Bread (standard loaf): $0.33

Potatoes (5 lb bag): $0.59

Hellmann's mayonnaise: $1.39

Campbell's tomato soup (10.75 oz can): $0.10

Fresh strawberries (per pound): $0.31

Ground beef (per pound): $0.98

Sugar (5 lb bag): $0.50

Fig Newton cookies (1 lb package): $0.39

Fruit cocktail (can): $0.20

Dozen eggs: $0.52

Gallon of milk: $1.20

We deliver fresh tomato flavor.
M'm! M'm! Good!

Hawaiian Punch Fruit Juice (12 oz can): $0.12

Coca-Cola or Pepsi (6 pack of 12 oz cans): $0.69

Kodak Pocket camera: $28.00

Columbia Hi-Rise children's bicycle: $36.88

Barbie Doll Designer Collection: from $2.85

Basketball: $6.99

Frisbee: $0.94

Men's Wrangler jeans: $12.00

Men's suit: $70.00

Men's regular dress shirt: $6.99

Roxanne Ladies Swimsuit: $30.00

Ladies Timex watch: $30.00

Ladies Deirdra wig: $20.00

Ladies front slit dress: $18.00

Mattress (twin size): $34.50

Classic Cook Center: $474.95

White Contemporary Dinette Set: $282.95

Maytag Deluxe clothes dryer: $119.00

Maytag Deluxe washing machine: $169.00

Joy dishwashing liquid (1 quart bottle): $0.75

Vornado lawn mower: $59.97

Rose bush: $1.49

Aspirin for children (bottle with 36 pills): $0.26

Johnson & Johnson Band Aids (packet with 60 units) $0.46

Sucrets throat lozenges (box with 24 lozenges): $0.44

Listerine mouthwash (14 oz bottle): $0.67

Ivory soap (pack of 4 bars): $0.29

Norelco hair dryer: $10.99

Movie ticket (national average): $1.50

LP vinyl record: $0.49

Stereo radio: $89.88

Wrangler thinks Americans spend too much for clothes.

Wrangler Jeans & Mr. Wrangler Sportswear

Emerson Permacolor. It's tuned in before you turn it on.

EMERSON

Emerson 19" black and white television: $98.00

Cruise to Bermuda (7 days): $575.00 per person

Tuition at Harvard University: $2.800 per year

Daily newspaper (national average): $0.15

First-class stamp: $0.10

These were some of the leading census and economic indicators for the UK in 1972:

Population: 56,096,677

Life expectancy: 72.12 years

Public net debt (as total percent of GDP): 50.72

Inflation: 7.13%

Consumer Price Index: 22.5

Unemployment: 4.3%

FTSE All-Share Index (high): 222.18

These were the median prices for selected products and assets in the United Kingdom in 1972:

TV license for black and white television: £7

TV license for color television: £12

Ferguson 24" black & white TV: £67.00

Pye 22" color TV: £239.00

Omega Swiss watch: £32.50

Seiko Japanese quartz watch: £24.95

Gallon of petrol: 35p

New car: Ford Cortina: £1,022.00 | Mini 850: £695 | Fiat 500: £650

Bottle of Haig whisky: £2.52

Bottle of Harvey's Bristol Cream sherry: £1.25

Pint of beer: 14-18p

Pack of 20 cigarettes: 26½p

Pint of milk: 5p

White 1¾ lb wrapped and sliced loaf of bread: 10p

St Ivel Golden Meadow ½ lb butter: 11½p

Maxwell House 4oz coffee: 25p

Bag of Golden Wonder crisps: 3p

One dozen large white eggs: 22p

Cod cost (per pound): 33p

Haddock (per pound): 35p

Kippers (per pound): 21p

Average house price: £7,000.00

Daily newspaper (average): 3p

Tracy's Tea Party toy set: £6.28

Monopoly board game: £1.35

Long-playing (LP) record: 77p to £2.25

Women's trouser suit with spotted cravat from C&A: £8.95

Women's tights from Woolworth's: 15-29p

Men's pair of socks from Woolworth's: 25p

Men's drip-dry nylon shirts from Woolworth's: £1.25

Men's paisley patterned polyester/cotton shirt from C&A: £1.65

Men's suit made to measure from Burton: £19.50

Men's shower-proof topcoat from Burton: £17.50

* * *

Made in the USA
Monee, IL
08 February 2022

90892107R00049